The House I Become

Twenty-One Windows into a Life Unfolding

Jay K. Singh

India | USA | UK

Copyright © Jay K. Singh
All Rights Reserved.

This book has been self-published with all reasonable efforts taken to make the material error-free by the author. No part of this book shall be used, reproduced in any manner whatsoever without written permission from the author, except in the case of brief quotations embodied in critical articles and reviews.

The Author of this book is solely responsible and liable for its content including but not limited to the views, representations, descriptions, statements, information, opinions, and references ["Content"]. The Content of this book shall not constitute or be construed or deemed to reflect the opinion or expression of the Publisher or Editor. Neither the Publisher nor Editor endorse or approve the Content of this book or guarantee the reliability, accuracy, or completeness of the Content published herein and do not make any representations or warranties of any kind, express or implied, including but not limited to the implied warranties of merchantability, fitness for a particular purpose.

The Publisher and Editor shall not be liable whatsoever...

Made with ❤ on the BookLeaf Publishing Platform
www.bookleafpub.in
www.bookleafpub.com

Dedication

For the hands that left light on my walls—
and for the rooms I didn't know were mine
until I opened them.

Preface

I didn't set out to write a book. I set out to keep myself company.

For twenty-one mornings I made tea, stood by the same window, and tried to tell the truth in a small, useful way. Some days the lines came like rain; most days they came like taps that needed patient turning. I promised myself one page, not a perfect one—just a page that could hold what the day had already begun to say.

If you and I were neighbors, this is what you'd notice from the street: the lamp goes on before dawn; a kettle argues; a single figure at the window, barefoot, not yet speaking. Inside, the small things keep me honest. **The key** on its hook asks me what I want to open. **Light** slides up the wall and refuses to be hurried. **Salt** remembers last night's meal and, somehow, my grandmother's hands. **Shoes** wait by the door, polite, patient, daring. A **train** faraway names the city out loud. I didn't choose these as symbols. They chose me as their anchor. In the mornings I was lost, I wrote one of them down and kept walking.

These poems were written daily and in order. They know

each other. The first seven listen more than they speak. The middle ones start calling things by their names. The last ones loosen their shoulders and carry what they've learned without showing off. Somewhere in the middle a line returned to me and wouldn't leave: *I am becoming my own address.*It isn't a slogan. It's a quiet practice—standing where I am and letting that be enough room to begin.

If this book has a plot, it is ordinary: making tea, opening a window, choosing which door is mine today, forgiving what I can't redo, loving the people who are right here. I wanted the poems to earn their warmth. No grand pronouncements, just a steady light you can read by. Sometimes I fail at that and reach; sometimes I manage to stay close to the floor where life is actually happening—on tile, on sidewalk, on bus steps, on temple stairs.

I hope you don't read these pages for instruction. Read them the way you'd watch a neighbor water a plant—half for the plant, half for the way a person learns to be gentle over time. Read them out loud if you can. Take one with you to the kitchen or the train or the long hallway between two hard conversations. Skip, circle back, underline the line that leans your way. If a poem doesn't speak to you, let it pass; another might. If one does, put it in your pocket. Carry it until it turns warm.

Thank you for opening this book. Thank you for bringing your life to meet mine at the window. If we do this right, you'll leave each poem a little more inside your own house. And if, somewhere along the way, you find yourself touching your keys and thinking, *yes, this one—* then we've both written something true.

— JKS

Acknowledgements

This book is a house I didn't build alone.

To my first readers—who told me where the walls held and where the drafts whistled—thank you for your candor and tenderness.

To the poets and teachers who taught me to listen before I touched the line, I am standing on your patient work.

To the editors and designers who gave this manuscript its good bones, and to the booksellers who put it into warm hands, I'm grateful for your craft.

To the friends who fed me tea and time while I wrote one page a day, your faith kept the lamp burning.

To the city that wakes early and refuses to apologize for its noise: you're the metronome in these lines.

To my family—who let me be quiet when I needed to hear—thank you for being my first address.

And to every reader who found a line on the internet and carried it here—your messages, shares, and small kindnesses made this book more possible than you know.

May these pages repay you with a window that opens when you need it.

Prologue

Key on the hook

The key hangs where I left it:
A small moon by the door, patient.

Night loosens its laces; the room remembers
How my shoes learned the shape of leaving.

On the counter: a salt ring from yesterday's tea,
A bright, ordinary compass.

Light tests the wall the way a friend might—
Gentle knock, no hurry, still sure.

Somewhere a train spells the city in iron.
I don't board. Not yet. I listen.

I touch the key. It is not a promise, only a hinge.
I am not a destination, only a door.

Between breath and handle, a house pauses—
And then, very softly, gives me back my name.

1. The Street Window

At 5:12 the city is already speaking—
A low throat-clear of buses, a scooter's needle,
Someone dragging yesterday down the stairs.

My window keeps its thin promise of glass.
I lean close. The world fogs, then clears,
Like a chest learning the shape of breath.

Across the lane, a woman salts a pan with her fingers,
Snow in small rehearsals. A boy ties his left shoe twice.
A shop shutter unrolls like a prayer mat.

I check my pockets for the key that is not lost,
Touch metal to name the morning mine.
Light climbs the opposite wall, a careful animal.

News vendors throw headlines like flat stones.
A train answers from far inside the city—
Iron syllables, practiced and late.

My tea decides to boil rather than whisper.
The kettle mouth brightens into a small warning.
Steam writes what I won't say yet.

I count how many doors I could open if I began,
Then stand still and count again.
Salt on my tongue, window on my skin.

The woman across turns her wrist, turns the day.
The boy stands, knots certain.
Somewhere a switch goes down, and the street exhales.

I lift the latch half-way—
Morning leaning in, me leaning back—
Two shoulders learning the weight of a house.

2. Kitchen Light at 5:12

The switch clicks like a small throat clearing.
Square of light on tile, the room shrugging itself awake.

I stand where the warmth begins. The kettle, faithful animal,
Leans into a quiet shiver. Steam rehearses the day in cursive.

On the table: yesterday's salt ring,
A moon that stayed to witness what I forgot to say.

My hands learn the cup again—ear, lip, weight—
Ordinary liturgy, heat traveling bone to bone.

Shoes wait by the door, polite as questions.
The key blinks from its hook, unblaming.

Outside, a scooter dials the street to louder;
Far off, the train spells a promise I'm not taking yet.

I crack the window just enough for the morning to answer.
Light climbs the wall, careful, like someone who knows the stairs.

The first sip is a map I've drawn before and misplaced.
I follow it anyway—tongue to salt, breath to chest, chest to name.

No miracles, only what holds: tile, kettle, light.
I practice choosing it. I let it choose me back.

Somewhere a pan receives water; somewhere a wrist turns.
I keep still long enough to hear it—
The day placing both hands on the counter, saying: begin.

3. Unread messages

My phone wakes before I do.
It brings the sea to the bedside—
Small tides of names I know by weather.

I turn it face-down. The room keeps breathing.
Light works quietly at the wall,
The way someone who loves me puts on tea.

There are words waiting, and their shadows:
The joke I could finish,
The apology drafted like a bridge I don't cross,
The question that only wants a window, not an answer.

I'm learning the difference between silence and hiding.
One is a room with air.
The other is a locked drawer with my hand still in it.

A salt ring on the table remembers last night better than I do.
The key stays cool on its hook—no verdict.

Shoes keep their patience at the door.

I read the previews without opening the day too wide.
Someone sends a photo of rain;
Someone sends the kind of good news that needs a voice.
Someone sends nothing, which is also a kind of message.

I type: *Here.* I do not send it.
I type: *Tell me when you're ready.* I let it float, unsaid,
Like a paper boat I launch and keep.

Breath writes on the window and fades.
I practice being present without proof.
I let the train call the city from far away and decide not to board.

What I answer, I answer with my body:
Kettle on, cup in hand, a breath I don't rush.
What I don't, I place gently back on the shore.

I turn the phone over and choose one true reply.
I say only what I can carry to the sink and back.
The rest can wait in their soft blue envelopes.

Some mornings victory looks like this:
A thumb that doesn't argue with itself,
A door I open in the room I'm already in.

I rinse the cup. Light keeps at its small, faithful work.
The day doesn't demand a speech.
It asks for my name, and gets it.

4. The mirror doesn't blink

Before the kettle, before the street—
I meet the glass that knows me anyway.

It keeps its weather. I keep mine.
We don't hurry.

Light climbs the wall and lays a square on my shoulder,
Like someone placing a hand to say: stay.

I count the small fidelities:
The scar that never learned to apologize,
The stubborn curl, the sleep-mark crossing my cheek
Like a note from a kinder teacher.

The mirror doesn't blink when I do.
It holds the flinch and the breath after the flinch.
We practice calling this a face and not a project.

Salt at the lip where I bit down on a dream.
A pulse in the neck I didn't ask to keep time.

How quietly the body returns me to myself.

Shoes wait by the door, patient as ever.
The key hangs, cool as a thought I can choose.

Somewhere a train names the city out loud.
Not today, I tell it, and it keeps going.

I try one truth in a voice I can stand:
I am not a problem; I am a person.
The glass holds still, the way a friend holds still.

I touch the place under the eye I've learned to forgive.
Steam ghosts the corner, writes, then vanishes.
No miracle—only what stays when I don't look away.

I wipe the print I left and leave the rest.
The day waits on the other side of the door.
I put on my face like a key in a palm,
Turn once, and go.

5. Shoes by the Door

They wait where I left them—
Quiet animals facing east.

The mat remembers every hallway I've come home from,
Keeps a small country of grit under its tongue.

Light finds the laces first,
A thin river along the loops, steady as a pulse.

I stand barefoot for a while,
Learning the weather of this threshold.

The key hangs to my right, cool and ordinary,
A promise no louder than metal.

On the table a salt ring holds last night in place.
The kettle clicks; the window names the morning by breath.

I try a question I can answer with walking:

Today, is the door a gate or a guard?

Shoes don't argue. They offer a shape for leaving
And a way to return in the same language.

I sit to tie. The knot is the smallest prayer I know—
Don't let me come undone where I can help it.

Outside, a train says the city out loud and keeps going.
I let it practice being urgent so I don't have to.

One foot, then the other. The floor receives me.
The room does not take it personally.

I touch the key to check that I'm allowed. I am.
Light climbs the wall like a steady friend.

I open the door as if it were a sentence I'm ready to say.
The shoes translate me to street.

If anyone asks what victory looks like,
I will think of this—
How softly I left,
How easy it was to come back.

6. Rain on the Grill

The rain arrives like someone who knows the house,
Goes straight to the balcony, speaks in the thin bars.

Each drop a small metal note—
A typewriter I didn't mean to start.

I move the shoes back from the splash zone,
Leave their damp half-moons on the tile.

The key stays cool on its hook,
Patient as a thought I can return to.

Last night's salt dries pale on a plate;
Rain writes its own answer on the window and erases it.

Light loosens, becomes a softer animal,
Pads across the wall and sits.

Far off, a train says the city's name twice,
As if checking it hasn't changed.

I hold my cup under the leak that always finds the
corner,
Let the rim learn rain's handwriting.

What needed washing lets itself be washed:
Grit from the mat, the sharp from a sentence I regret.

I don't make a speech. I stand inside the sound.
The room breathes easier and so do I.

When the sky runs out of argument,
The grill keeps dripping in slow agreement.

I open the latch and leave it there—
A small hinge practicing forgiveness.

7. A Call I Don't Make

I carry the number to the window
Like a glass of water I'm not sure I can hold.

The phone is a small blue door.
I put my hand on the knob and let it rest there.

Light lifts its square onto the table,
An honest witness that doesn't offer advice.

On the plate: a faint salt ring,
Last night's weather drying itself without permission.

Shoes wait by the door, fluent in leaving.
The key hangs, unblaming, a cool sentence I don't have
to say.

Far off, a train practices the city's name.
I do not board; the morning is full enough.

I try the first line out loud to the room—

It shakes like a bridge someone forgot to finish.

What would I ask for anyway—
A new past, a softer echo, proof?

Steam from the cup writes and vanishes on the glass.
I learn from it: appear, be true, then go.

Instead of calling, I place the phone face down
Like I'm setting a small mercy on the counter.

I wash the cup. I rinse the ache.
I let the unsaid be tender and alive.

The door is still a door when I don't use it.
I touch the key to remember I could.

Light keeps working at the wall, patient as a friend.
The day hears me choose it and answers back.

8. The Train That's Always Late

It begins as a rumor under the morning,
A thin iron promise that keeps shifting its mouth.

I pour water like I'm learning to be slower.
Steam rehearses and leaves. Light does its patient work.

On the plate, the salt ring has turned into a small moon,
Proof that something stayed while I slept.

Shoes wait by the door, not hurrying me.
The key hangs where it always does—cool, available, kind.

I check the time I said I'd be ready.
The train ignores that time the way rain ignores roofs.

Across the lane someone rolls a shutter with their whole body.
I remember doors ask for shoulders, not schedules.

If it comes now, I will go.
If it doesn't, I will still arrive somewhere I can name.

The window fogs and clears; I practice with it—
Appear, soften, return.

I make space for the message that doesn't need a phone:
Breathe here. tend here. finish tying the left shoe twice.

A sparrow edits the silence. The kettle agrees.
Far off, the city says itself and waits to see if I repeat it.

I hear the platform inside my chest—
The announcements I can stop believing, the ones I can keep.

I say the line that keeps choosing me:
I am becoming my own address.

Not a headline. A practice.
Not arrival. A way to stand and mean it.

When the train finally leans into the day,
I'm not late. I'm ready.

I lock the door the tender way,

Key turning once like a throat clearing.

Light walks with me down the hall.
The shoe finds the first step and says, "*Go*".

9. Salt Jar

It sits near the stove like an elder—
Glass body, white weather, a lid that remembers every palm.

I lift it with both hands.
On the counter, light breaks into small islands.

Pinch and taste. My mouth finds a room with old furniture:
A voice that never measured, only knew.

Last night's ring halos the plate,
A quiet moon that stayed because I didn't.

The jar holds more than it looks like—
Grief that learned to be seasoning,
Laughter that never asked for a recipe.

I hear her say, "*Enough!*"—not as a warning,
As a blessing that fits in two fingers.

Shoes wait by the door, polite as always.
The key keeps its cool on the hook, loyal metal.

The train is a rumor again, spelling the city from far off.
I let it call. I answer here.

I salt the water before it knows it needs it,
The way I try to name what's coming
Before it turns into ache.

Steam lifts and writes, then vanishes.
Some things are truer after they've gone.

What I can't fix, I can flavor—
Make it honest, make it enough to carry.

I rinse the jar with care I wish I'd learned sooner,
Wipe the threads, set the lid down soft.

A few grains stay on my fingers.
I press them to my tongue, and I am held—
Kitchen, morning, a life that keeps its promises quietly.

Light stands with me at the counter.
I put the jar back where it waits without impatience.

When I leave, I'll touch the key like a thank-you.
For now, I season the day and taste it once,
Then once more, to be sure.

10. Inbox: Drafts

There is a folder where the versions of me live—
Not ghosts, just careful voices waiting for my breath.

Subject lines like small doors:
"I'm sorry about the Tuesday you carried alone."
"I don't need you to answer this."
"I'm here when the room is quieter."

I open one and the light on the desk leans in,
Not to judge, just to see if my hands are steady.

On the plate: a faint salt ring,
Proof that something stayed while we couldn't.

The phone hums like a nervous animal.
I stroke its back by not touching it.

Some drafts are bridges I almost finished.
Some are rooms with chairs no one sat in.
Some are single words—*Here.*

I keep folding and unfolding them like a note in class.

Shoes wait by the door, patient with the pace of my honesty.
The key on the hook glints, a quiet permission.

Far off, a train says the city out loud.
I let it practice urgency so I don't have to.

I read back to myself:
The lines I wrote when I was brave for a minute,
The ones I wrote when I mistook noise for truth,
The one that still feels like a window.

I don't need to send everything I mean.
Meaning doesn't vanish just because it is held.

I draft one more—no defense, no flourish:
"I hope today puts a gentle hand on your shoulder."
I save it like water in a glass beside the bed.

Steam writes on the pane and leaves—
Lessons and mercy in the same gesture.

What I do send, I can carry to the sink and back.
What I don't, I place where it can breathe.

I close the folder without scolding myself.
Light keeps its small, faithful job.

I touch the key, then let it hang.
The door is still a door; I'll use it when I mean to.

For now, I lace one shoe, then the other,
And walk the quiet distance between what I wrote
And what I'm ready to say.

11. Temple steps

I take the long way on purpose—
Past the tailor's gate, past the neem tree that keeps a green shoulder
For sparrows to practice arrival.

The steps begin before the door.
The stones that remember every heel,
Warm already with other people's prayers.

Shoes wait at the bottom like good listeners.
I leave them there, two quiet boats turned to shore.

Light moves down the corridor the way a hand
Moves down a back—no hurry, all consent.

I carry no flowers, only what I can't say yet.
At the tap I rinse my hands; the water forgets my name
And returns it clean.

On my tongue: a grain of last night's salt,

Memory showing me how small a sacrament can be.

A bell tests the air and the air agrees.
Somewhere a train spells the city in iron;
Its syllables wobble, then keep going.
Not this platform, I tell my chest. Not today.

I stand where the stone cools the heat I brought.
The key in my pocket is heavy enough to count as truth.
I touch it and it touches back: you can go home from here.

Inside, the god is quiet in a way I can bear—
Not answers, just the kind of listening
That makes your shoulders drop their guard.

I practice breathing like it's a language.
On the wall, light writes the oldest vowel.
A priest passes with a plate of flame;
The room brightens without becoming a performance.

I give what I have: two coins of attention,
A whispered apology I'm not ready to mail,
The names of people who need a softer morning.

When I step back into ordinary sun,
The sparrows don't make a big deal, and I love them for

it.

At the foot of the steps my shoes wait,
Faithful as a promise I can keep.
I tie the knot like a small bow to the day.

I put the key away, which is also a prayer.
The train is still somewhere else, late on purpose.
I take the road that smells like turmeric and rain.

If someone asks what happened, I'd say:
"Nothing changed"; but enough did I.
Stone under my feet, light on my shoulder,
A door in me opening without noise.

12. The plant I forgot to water

It greets me without drama—
A soft collapse, leaves holding the shape of a yes
They couldn't keep overnight.

I touch the soil and it answers in dust.
I tell it, "*I'm sorry*" - in the language of a cup.

Light steps onto the sill like a late friend.
We both pretend we weren't worried.

I carry the pot to the sink,
Let the first pour go straight through—
Soil drinking like someone who remembers how.

On the table a pale salt ring keeps last night's moon.
The kettle warms its throat but waits.

Shoes stand by the door, patient as ever.
The key hangs unblaming, cool as permission.

Far off, a train practices the city's name.
I let it call; I answer here.

The leaves lift a little, then a little more—
Forgiveness rehearsing its posture.

I drain the tray, wipe the lip, turn the pot
So the shy side meets the light.
We are both allowed to face a better window.

Steam writes on the glass and vanishes.
Some mercies arrive exactly that way.

I promise what I can keep:
Not perfection, just a hand on the morning,
A thumb testing soil before it asks.

I set the plant back where it lives,
Tuck the stray leaf behind its green ear.

The room exhales. I do too.
Nothing heroic—only water, only light.

If someone asks what love looks like today,
I will point here: a cup refilled,

A small thing standing up again,
The door still a door, and me choosing it slowly.

13. Neighborhood dog

He waits at the corner before I do,
Brown with a white sock, tail that knows my name.

We've never scheduled this,
But both of us keep showing up.

I tap my pocket out of habit—key cool as truth,
Shoes learning the pace of a gentle morning.

He blinks the way old friends blink:
No questions, just room.

Light takes the curb first,
Lays a small gold hand on his ribs.

I hold out a palm that remembers salt.
He reads it, decides I'm welcome,
Leans his head into the space between my knees.

Somewhere a train says the city out loud.

Neither of us turns. We are practicing a different urgency.

The kettle man across the lane knocks cups together.
Steam lifts like a simple blessing.
I crumble half a biscuit; he eats like he's listening.

A scooter rides past, loud and brief.
The dog doesn't audition for alarm.
He is the size of the street's calm.

There's a cut on his ear, healing into a story
He doesn't need to tell me.
I scratch the place that stayed soft anyway.

Light climbs my sleeve, then his back.
We are both warm enough to begin.

When I leave, he doesn't follow—
Doesn't make my going about him.
He turns three slow circles and lies down in the square
The sun has chosen.

I touch the key in my pocket to remember I can return.
I do not hurry the shoelaces.
I carry a little of his unafraid with me.

By the time the train speaks our block's name again,
I am already home enough to answer.

And in that quiet, I hear him still,
A heartbeat lingering under the asphalt,
A whisper between moments,
Reminding me the world is wide,
That love's patience is a thread,
Woven in the fabric of arrival and departure,
Holding us close even in absence.

14. Laundry on the Line

I carry the wet basket to the balcony
And the morning takes two steps closer.

Soap still in the air, a little bright faith.
My wrists learn the weight and the letting go.

Light threads itself through cotton,
Makes flags out of shirts that have nothing to prove.

I pinch the first clothespin the way a truth is held—
Not tight, just enough to stay.

Salt dries in the seams where yesterday leaned.
The wind reads the hems and nods yes, yes.

Shoes wait inside the door, polite, drip-free.
The key hangs on its hook like a pause I can keep.

Across the lane, a neighbor's line answers mine—
Parallel rivers in a language our mothers taught us.

Far off, the train spells the city and then the silence after.
I let it pass; these names need sun, not departure.

A shirt balloons and finds its own breath.
A pillowcase takes the shape of a soft argument and
releases it.

I smooth a stubborn collar, apology in my fingertips.
I turn a dark garment inside out so it keeps what it is.

Steam ghosts the window and vanishes—
Lessons I'm finally learning while my hands are busy.

There are small fidelities in this work:
Pairing the socks that forgave each other,
Untying the trouser leg that taught itself a knot.

I think of the words I didn't send and how clean they feel
Just hanging here, moving without being thrown.

Light keeps stitching across the line,
A quiet seam I won't unpick.

When the breeze lifts everything at once,
I stand still and count to three—
Enough time to be a person who can let what's damp

become sky.

I leave the basket empty and call it progress.
The door is still a door when I enter again.

I touch the key to thank it for waiting.
Inside, the floor remembers my wet footprints and then forgets.

If anyone asks what forgiveness looks like today:
Cloth to sun, pins to palm,
And me not rushing the part where it takes time to dry.

15. Two tickets

They're on the table before we are—
Two paper doors, corners curled like commas,
Asking what we plan to put between them.

Light tries each edge and stays.
Beside them: the pale salt ring, last night's small moon,
A cup that knows our names by heat.

You read yours like a promise.
I read mine like a permission.
Both are true enough for morning.

Shoes wait by the door—four of them, patient,
Learning the language of walking together.

The key in my pocket is cool and ordinary.
I touch it and it touches back:
Home doesn't mind if we step out.

Far off, a train says the city out loud.

Today, for once, we answer.
Not for arrival—
But for the seat where our shoulders understand each other.

We don't match our reasons.
We match the rhythm: turn, lock, stairs, street.
You take the sunlight. I take the shade.
The tickets take us both.

At the barrier the paper gives itself up,
A soft click, a small eclipse punched in the corner.
Proof that there is a way to cross without announcing it.

On the platform, the wind invents a hymn from our sleeves.
When the train leans in late, it's still on time for us.

We sit facing forward but point out the side—
A city rehearsing its names on glass and brick.
You tap the window at the bakery you love.
I nod at the neem that keeps a green shoulder for birds.

We are not hurrying an answer.
We are agreeing on a view.

When we rise, the tickets, lighter now,

Fold into my pocket beside the key.
Home comes with us either way.

If someone asks what became of our plans,
I'll show them the two small holes in the paper,
The way your sleeve found my hand at the curve,
The door we'll open later with the same ease we left.

16. The long walk home

We step off where the station forgets our names.
    You lift a hand; it keeps waving inside me
    Long after we turn into separate streets.

    Evening knows the road better than I do.
    Light changes keys; doors learn dusk.
    My shoes negotiate with the pavement—
        Slow, then honest, then mine.

I carry what we said in the shallow pocket,
    What we didn't in the deep one.
    Both are heavier than a ticket,
        Lighter than a promise.

    A scooter stitches the lane to night.
Pressure cookers call to each other from windows.
Somewhere a train says the city again, farther this time.
    I let it keep my name safe and loud for later.

Salt at the mouth—sweat, maybe; maybe the day itself

Leaving a small handwriting on my skin.
I taste it and don't argue.

The neem we pass in mornings holds a shadow for me.
The neighborhood dog lifts his head,
Accepts my soft hello like we're both trying to be better.

I count the reasons to hurry and don't.
There is a way to return that doesn't erase the leaving.
I practice it one streetlight at a time.

Shoes ask nothing but next step, next step.
The key in my pocket does not insist;
It waits the way kindness waits—
Present, unafraid of my pace.

I think of the plant that forgave me,
Of the laundry learning wind,
Of the drafts I saved instead of sending,
How many rooms a day can be.

By the bakery, a girl laughs into the flour.
By the tailor, an old song mends the air.
I walk through other people's tenderness
Like someone allowed to.

When my building appears, smaller than the feeling,

I stop outside and let my breath arrive ahead of me.
No miracle, only what holds:
The latch, the mat, the light behind the curtain.

I touch the key and it touches me back.
Inside, the door will not ask for a speech.
It will open the way a good friend does—
Once, and then all the way.

I turn it, hear the small throat-clear of home.
Shoes loosen their grief.
Salt becomes memory instead of ache.

In the kitchen the kettle understands.
Steam writes and vanishes, as always.
I say my name out loud, softly,
Like a person I'm learning to trust.

This is the distance I needed—
Long enough to carry the day without breaking it,
Close enough to set it down and mean it.

17. A room without clocks

I choose the room that doesn't ask what time it is.
The phone sleeps in another mouth of the house,
Face down, learning to be quiet.

Light becomes the only measure—
Moving its small gold shoulder across the wall,
Teaching the floor where afternoon begins.

Shoes sigh open by the door,
Sentences I don't have to finish.
The key rests on the table, cool as consent.

On a plate, the faint salt ring from last night's tea
Keeps its pale moon without reminding me of anything.
I touch it anyway, to remember staying is also a motion.

Steam rises from the kettle, writes, vanishes—
A practice I try with my thoughts.
Come. Be true. Go.

The plant on the sill doesn't count.
It leans toward what it knows and is forgiven.
I follow it by breathing until numbers fall off the edges.

Somewhere a train spells the city in iron;
I let its urgency pass through my ribs
Like weather that doesn't belong to this room.

I sit on the floor so the floor can hold me.
Scar, heartbeat, quiet—
Fidelities that do not need a clock to exist.

I think of what I could be late for and am not:
The apology I can only write when I'm kind,
The door I can open without leaving.

In this room I don't rehearse my life;
I live the part where no one is watching.
I let the light touch my shoulder and call it proof.

When I stand, the day is whatever it is.
I lace my shoes with a soft grip,
Return the key to my pocket like a promise I can keep.

I don't check a face made of numbers.
I check the window: yes. The world is here.

I open the door the way a good friend answers—once, and all the way.

18. The book I meant to write

The one I kept in the pocket with quiet worry.
The one that began with a **window** and refused to apologize for light.
The one where the **kettle** knew the plot before I did.
The one that let a **key** be only metal until I touched it.
The one that used **salt** for truth, not for wounds.
The one whose **shoes** were tied slowly, then well.
The one that heard the **train** and didn't have to run.
The one where **forgiveness** talked like a neighbor and brought tea.
The one that didn't make me a lesson to love me.
The one with a sink that understood rinsing.
The one that said *begin* without a trumpet.
The one in which I didn't call because silence was a room, not a wall.
The one where the **mirror** held still long enough for my face to catch up.
The one that let a **plant** fail and stand again without shame.

The one that put **two tickets** on the table and chose company over certainty.

The one that knew **laundry** dries on its own schedule, so do hearts.

The one that spelled the city in iron and chose my street anyway.

The one that kept drafts like birds on a wire—near, undecided, alive.

The one that understood how a bell tests air and air says yes.

The one where grief learned to measure softer.

The one that let my name arrive from the inside.

The one with a **door** I opened because I wanted to, not because I had to.

The one that said: *You do not owe the day a performance.*

The one that sat on the floor until numbers fell off the edges.

The one that made a room from breath and called it home.

The one that used soup, and lists, and ordinary mornings for structure.

The one that returned to the **refrain** without turning it into a slogan.

The one that loved a **neighborhood dog** and meant it.

The one that kept a small moon on a plate and never forced it to be a metaphor.

The one that chose a softer word when the sharp one wasn't true.

The one where I tied the left shoe twice and called it wisdom.

The one that didn't rush the apology, only made space for it.

The one that let **light** move the plot across a wall.

The one that used ***Here*** as a complete sentence.

The one that remembered my grandmother's hands without asking them to work again.

The one that swapped urgency for presence and didn't miss anything.

The one that understood victory could look like a thumb not sending.

The one where *I am becoming my own address* arrived as practice, not headline.

The one you could read in a kitchen, standing, with steam on your face.

The one I'm writing now, line by line, instead of promising later.

And if I can't write that book today—
I will write this line, and let it hold the door.

19. When Light Switches Sides

It happens so quietly I almost miss it—
The square on the wall loosens its grip,
Packs its gold, and walks across the room.
Afternoon trades hands with evening.
Everything learns a softer edge.
I'm at the sink, wrist in warm water,
Salt lifting from the plate like a small apology.
Steam writes and lets go, as always.
Shoes rest by the door, tongues open,
Breathing out the day they carried.
The key waits on the hook, cool as consent.
I touch it the way a thought checks if it's true.
Outside, a scooter stitches the lane to dusk;
Somewhere a train says the city's name lower,
As if not to wake anyone.
Light climbs the opposite wall,
Lays a gentle palm on my shoulder, then moves on.
I follow it without leaving.
This is the hour that forgives hard lines—

The mirror lets my face belong to itself,
The plant keeps its shape without trying.
If there is a lesson, let it be small:
What was bright over here can be bright over there,
And nothing breaks to make that happen.
I set a cup down where morning used to sit.
It looks right here too.
A draft I didn't send becomes a window;
I open nothing and it still feels like air.
I think of the rooms I've learned to carry,
How many of them turn tender at this angle.
Shoes are not asking for a plan;
They are asking for presence, step by step.
I tell them: maybe later. They understand.
The key does not take it personally.
It waits, certain of a door either way.
Light reaches the shelf, touches the old receipt,
The note with two names, the spare button.
Everything common gets a moment of choir.
I stand still long enough to be here.
No performance, just the lid on the jar
Closing without a sound.
When the last stripe leaves the wall,
The room is not poorer—only honest.
I switch on the lamp the way a friend answers a call:
Once, and all the way.
The train passes—late on purpose.

I don't follow. I let the evening keep what it knows.
If someone asks what changed, I'll say:
The light, and therefore the room,
And therefore me—
Not different, only truer on this side.

20. Keys in my pocket

They're heavier today—
Not by metal, by meaning.
I slide them in and the fabric understands:
Here is what opens, here is what I am allowed.

The ring makes its small music when I walk,
A quiet cousin of a bell agreeing with the air.
Light tests the hallway, shoulder to shoulder with me.
We make a pair the building knows.

On the table a pale salt ring keeps last night honest.
I touch it to remember that staying counts too.

Shoes wait by the door, tongues soft,
Not asking where, only if I'm ready to be there.

Somewhere a train screams the city out loud.
I let it carry my name for later.
For now, I carry these.

I map each tooth with my thumb—
Front door, gate, cupboard with the good plates,
A small brass lamp I keep meaning to try.

In my pocket, they warm to my temperature,
Like choices I've practiced long enough to trust.

I think of the doors I haven't opened
Because the question wasn't true yet.
I think of the ones I closed gently
And how those rooms kept blessing me anyway.

Steam writes and vanishes on the window.
I learn the trick again: appear, be true, go.

I walk to the door and don't perform.
No speech, no proof. Just a person with keys.

The knob understands my hand.
The lock clears its throat and yields.

If anyone asks what victory looks like,
I'll show them this weight—
The ordinary kind that doesn't bruise,
The kind that sounds like home when it moves.

I put the keys back in my pocket,

Carry the sound down the stairs.
Light comes with me, faithful as a friend.

Outside, the morning is exactly itself.
I choose it with the soft click I've earned.

Somewhere the train is late on purpose.
I am not. I am here—
Keys warm, salt honest on my tongue,
Shoes ready to make the road remember me.

The wind plays a song I know by heart,
Whispering promises wrapped in possibility.

Each step echoes where I've been,
A rhythmic goodbye to yesterday's shadows.

I breathe in deeply, savoring the freshness,
The taste of dawn lingering like a secret.

I watch the world unfold, each moment a canvas,
Painted anew with the brush of my intent.

Here, in the quiet, I gather the loose threads of hope,
Knots of ambition shining just beneath the surface.

I feel the paths ahead, drawn like lines in the air,

Waiting for footprints to mark their intended way.

With each stride, I stitch my story into the fabric,
Indelible impressions woven with care.

Yes, I am here—
A chorus of keys jingling softly,
The echoes of my heart resonating in the dawn.

21. Open Window, Open Mouth

I open the window the way a friend answers a knock—
Once, and all the way.

Air steps in without shoes.
Curtain lifts its small hymn; light puts a warm hand on my shoulder.

On the table, the pale salt ring keeps last night kind.
The kettle clears its throat and doesn't insist.

I stand where the warmth begins and try the softest courage: *breathe.*
The breath writes what it knows and lets it go.

The key in my pocket is cool and certain.
It doesn't tell me what to do. It reminds me I can.

Somewhere a train screams the city out loud.
For the first time I answer without leaving.

I taste the rim of the cup—salt, heat, morning.
My tongue remembers the road to my name.

Shoes wait by the door, patient as ever.
They will answer me if I ask. They will bless me if I stay.

The mirror gives me back a face I can stand.
I practice saying one true thing, then another.

I am becoming my own address.

The room doesn't need a speech.
It needs a person to arrive and mean it.

Light crosses the floor and finds my mouth.
I let it. I let myself.

Window open, mouth open—
The day and I agree to start from here.

I touch the key, then let it rest.
I tie the left shoe twice, or not at all.

Either way, the world is here.
Either way, I can carry it in my voice.

Coda

House of after

The rooms remember without asking—
A thin moon of salt on the plate,
Steam's old handwriting on the glass,
Two shoes turned toward home like good listeners.

The key sleeps in my pocket and is not a verdict.
When I touch it, it says only, "*If, when, yes*".

Light has learned the map of these walls.
It finds my shoulder by habit and rests there,
Not to fix me—only to stand with me
Until I remember how to breathe.

The train still names the city in iron.
Sometimes I answer, sometimes I let it keep my name for
when I'm ready to travel again.

This is the after that isn't an ending:
The plant on the sill lifting its forgiven leaves,
The laundry taking its time to become sky,
The mirror holding still while I practice being a person.

I make tea without ceremony.
I taste the rim—salt, heat, morning—
And say one true thing to the quiet, "*I'm here*".

There is no chorus, only small fidelities:
Unlocking the door as if it were a throat clearing,
Tying the left shoe twice because wisdom can be simple,
Placing the phone face down so my hands are free to hold.

The house learns me back.
It turns its hinges softly, opens without a speech.
Every ordinary object keeps faith at its own scale.

I do not promise forever. I promise this:
To meet the day where it stands,
To choose what holds—tile, kettle, light—
To let the rest arrive in its right size.

If you're looking for victory, it lives here now:
In a name spoken gently,
In keys that sound like home when they move,

In a window open enough to let the world in
And a mouth open enough to answer.

I am becoming my own address.
Not a headline. A practice.
I carry it room to room,
And the rooms carry me back.

www.ingramcontent.com/pod-product-compliance
Lightning Source LLC
Chambersburg PA
CBHW060350050426
42449CB00011B/2914